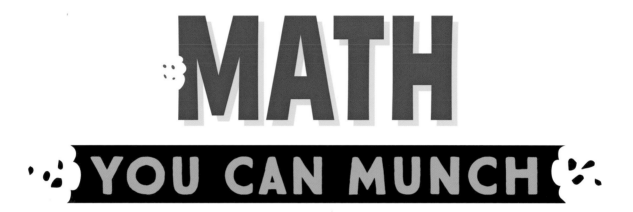

MATH
YOU CAN MUNCH

MEGAN BORGERT-SPANIOL

Consulting Editor, Diane Craig, MA/Reading Specialist

Super Sandcastle

An Imprint of Abdo Publishing
abdobooks.com

ABDOBOOKS.COM

Published by Abdo Publishing, a division of ABDO, PO Box 398166, Minneapolis, Minnesota 55439. Copyright © 2019 by Abdo Consulting Group, Inc. International copyrights reserved in all countries. No part of this book may be reproduced in any form without written permission from the publisher. Super SandCastle™ is a trademark and logo of Abdo Publishing.

Printed in the United States of America, North Mankato, Minnesota
102018
012019

THIS BOOK CONTAINS RECYCLED MATERIALS

Design: Emily O'Malley, Mighty Media, Inc.
Production: Mighty Media, Inc.
Editor: Liz Salzmann
Cover Photographs: Mighty Media, Inc.; Shutterstock
Interior Photographs: iStockphoto; Mighty Media, Inc.; Shutterstock; Wikimedia Commons

The following manufacturers/names appearing in this book are trademarks: Kellogg's® Froot Loops®, Kraft® Jet-Puffed®, M&M'S®, Nestle®, Pillsbury Creamy Supreme®, Pyrex®, Reese's® Pieces®, Reynolds®, Reynolds® Cut-Rite®, Sharpie®, Smucker's®, Voortman™

Library of Congress Control Number: 2018948865

Publisher's Cataloging-in-Publication Data

Names: Borgert-Spaniol, Megan, author.
Title: Math you can munch / by Megan Borgert-Spaniol.
Description: Minneapolis, Minnesota : Abdo Publishing, 2019 | Series: Super simple science you can snack on
Identifiers: ISBN 9781532117268 (lib. bdg.) | ISBN 9781532170126 (ebook)
Subjects: LCSH: Mathematics--Juvenile literature. | Cooking--Juvenile literature. | Science--Experiments--Juvenile literature. | Gastronomy--Juvenile literature.
Classification: DDC 641.0--dc23

Super SandCastle™ books are created by a team of professional educators, reading specialists, and content developers around five essential components—phonemic awareness, phonics, vocabulary, text comprehension, and fluency—to assist young readers as they develop reading skills and strategies and increase their general knowledge. All books are written, reviewed, and leveled for guided reading and early reading intervention programs for use in shared, guided, and independent reading and writing activities to support a balanced approach to literacy instruction.

TO ADULT HELPERS

The projects in this book are fun and simple. There are just a few things to remember to keep kids safe. Some projects require the use of sharp or hot objects. Also, kids may be using messy ingredients. Make sure they protect their clothes and work surfaces. Review the projects before starting, and be ready to assist when necessary.

KEY SYMBOLS

Watch for these warning symbols in this book. Here is what they mean.

HOT!
You will be working with something hot. Get help!

SHARP!
You will be working with something sharp. Get help!

CONTENTS

WHAT IS MATH?

EUCLID

Math is the science of numbers. Humans have been doing math for thousands of years. People who study math are called mathematicians. These people explore numbers in quantities, shapes, measurements, and more.

EUCLID

Greek **scholar** Euclid lived more than 2,000 years ago. He wrote a textbook on **geometry**. Geometry is math that deals with points, lines, angles, and shapes. Euclid's teachings formed the basis of geometry as we know it.

BLAISE PASCAL

BLAISE PASCAL

French mathematician Blaise Pascal is known for creating the first digital **calculator**. He invented it in the 1640s. The calculator, called the Pascaline, could add and subtract.

ADA LOVELACE

Ada Lovelace was an English mathematician. In 1843, she wrote an **algorithm**. It was for use on another early computing machine. Many historians consider her work to be the first computer program.

ADA LOVELACE

MATH TODAY

Math plays a major role in the modern world. Many mathematicians use computers to perform **complicated calculations**. This advanced math helps people forecast the weather, travel to space, and more.

WEATHER FORECASTING

The National Oceanic and Atmospheric Administration (NOAA) uses computers to perform many millions of calculations each second! The calculations help forecast the weather.

WEATHER COMPUTERS CAN SHOW WHAT THE WEATHER MAY BE LIKE FOR THE NEXT HOURS OR DAYS.

GPS

Have you looked up directions to a friend's house on a smartphone? This uses the Global Positioning System (GPS). GPS uses **geometry** to locate where you are in relation to where you are going!

PEOPLE COULD USE GPS ON PHONES STARTING IN THE EARLY 2000S.

SPACE TRAVEL

Math is used in every part of space travel. This includes **calculating** a spacecraft's speed, flight path, and more.

A SPACE SHUTTLE CONNECTS TO A SPACE STATION.

MATH SNACKS

You can learn a lot about math by making the fun snacks in this book!

GET READY

* Ask an adult for **permission** to use kitchen tools and ingredients.

* Read the snack's list of tools and ingredients. Make sure you have everything you need.

* Does a snack require ingredients you don't like? Get creative! Find other ingredients you enjoy instead.

SNACK CLEAN & SAFE

* Clean your work surface before you start.

* Wash your hands before you work with food.

* Keep your work area tidy. This makes it easier to find what you need.

* Ask an adult for help when handling sharp or hot objects.

CLEANING UP

* Don't waste unused ingredients! Store leftover ingredients to use later.

* Clean your work surface. Wash any dishes or tools you used.

* Wash your hands before you eat your snack!

INGReDIENTS & TooLS

BREAD

CHOCOLATE CHIPS

CHOCOLATE
FROSTING

FROOT LOOPS CEREAL

GRAHAM CRACKERS

JELLY

M&M'S CANDIES

MARSHMALLOW
FLUFF

NUTELLA

PEANUT BUTTER

PRETZEL STICKS

REESE'S PIECES
CANDIES

ROLL OF SUGAR
COOKIE DOUGH

VANILLA FROSTING

VANILLA WAFER
COOKIES

HERE ARE SOME OF THE INGREDIENTS AND TOOLS YOU WILL NEED TO MAKE THE SNACKS IN THIS BOOK.

BAKING SHEET

COOLING RACK

CUTTING BOARD

DINNER KNIFE

HOT GLUE GUN & GLUE STICKS

MEASURING CUPS

MICROWAVE-SAFE BOWL

NEWSPAPER

PARCHMENT PAPER

PLASTIC ZIPPER BAGS

PROTRACTOR

SHARP KNIFE

WAX PAPER

WOODEN DOWELS

WOODEN SKEWERS

TOOLS

SNACK ABACUS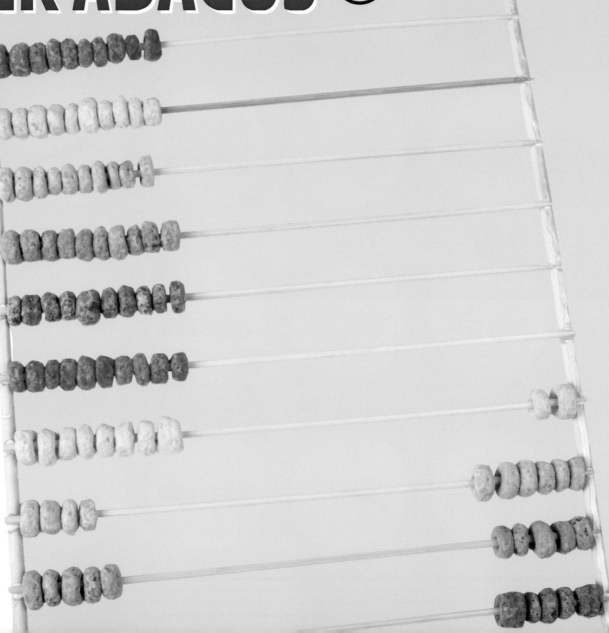

INGREDIENTS

- Froot Loops cereal

TOOLS

- 2 12-inch (30 cm) wooden dowels
- newspaper
- 10 wooden skewers
- ruler
- hot glue gun & glue sticks

12

The abacus was invented more than 2,000 years ago. It has beads arranged on rods. Users move the beads to perform **calculations**. Make a tasty abacus for math-ing and **munching**!

1. Lay a wooden dowel vertically on top of newspaper.

2. Set the skewers on the right side of the dowel. Place their left ends on top of the dowel. Space the skewers about 1 inch (2.5 cm) apart.

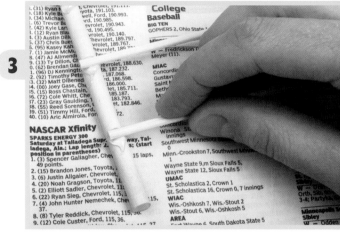

3. Hot glue the ends of the skewers to the dowel. Let the glue dry.

4. Slide ten Froot Loops onto the top skewer. All the Froot Loops should be the same color.

5. Choose a new color for the next skewer. Slide ten Froot Loops of that color onto the skewer.

6. Repeat step 5 for the rest of the skewers.

Continued on the next page.

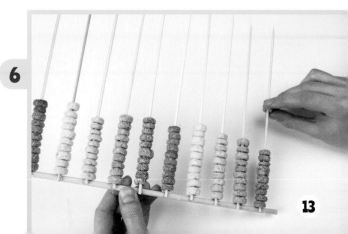

8

9

7. Push all of the Froot Loops to the left side of the abacus. Lay the abacus on newspaper.

8. Set the second wooden dowel next to the free ends of the skewers. Carefully spread hot glue along the dowel.

9. Press the ends of the skewers to the dowel. Keep them spaced 1 inch (2.5 cm) apart. Let the glue dry.

10. Use your tasty abacus to perform simple **calculations**! (See page 15.)

SCIENCE BITE

	BILLIONS
	HUNDRED MILLIONS
	TEN MILLIONS
	MILLIONS
	HUNDRED THOUSANDS
	TEN THOUSANDS
	THOUSANDS
	HUNDREDS
	TENS
	ONES

THIS ABACUS SHOWS THE NUMBER 51. THERE ARE FIVE BEADS ON THE RIGHT SIDE OF THE TENS ROW. THAT EQUALS 50. THERE IS ONE BEAD ON THE RIGHT SIDE OF THE ONES ROW. THAT EQUALS 1. THESE NUMBERS ADD UP TO 51.

CRUNCHING NUMBERS

INGREDIENTS

- graham cracker
- chocolate and vanilla frosting
- Reese's Pieces or M&M's candies

TOOLS

- cutting board
- sharp knife
- dinner knife
- spoon
- measuring cup
- 2 plastic zipper bags
- scissors

Calculators can help people solve simple or **complicated** math problems. Crunch numbers with this chewable calculator!

1. Have an adult help you cut about one-third off the length of the graham cracker. Spread chocolate frosting on the larger piece.

2. Seal ¼ cup vanilla frosting in a plastic bag. Cut a corner of the bag to make a small hole.

3. Gently **squeeze** the bag until frosting comes out of the hole. Use it to draw a rectangle near one end of the graham cracker. This is the calculator's screen.

4. Place four rows of four candies under the screen. These are the calculator's buttons. Use one color for the number buttons. Use a different color for the other buttons.

5. Seal ¼ cup chocolate frosting in a separate plastic bag. Cut a corner of the bag to make a small hole. Make the hole as small as possible.

6. Squeeze the bag of chocolate frosting to draw the numbers and **symbols** on the calculator buttons. Draw any number on the screen.

FRACTION COOKIES

FOURTHS

THIRDS

EIGHTHS

HALVES

INGREDIENTS

- roll of sugar cookie dough
- chocolate frosting

TOOLS

- parchment paper
- baking sheet
- sharp knife
- cutting board
- dinner knife
- oven mitts
- cooling rack
- measuring cup
- plastic zipper bag
- scissors

A fraction is part of a whole. Fractions are often shown using circles. Use cookies and frosting to make sweet fractions!

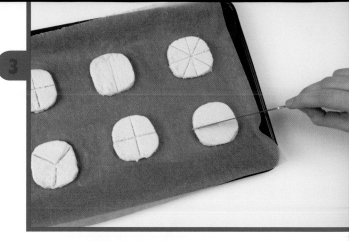

1. Put parchment paper on the baking sheet.

2. Have an adult help you cut the cookie dough into **slices**. Place the slices on the baking sheet.

3. Use a dinner knife to draw lines on the cookies to divide them into fractions. Make fractions from halves to eighths.

4. Have an adult help you bake the cookies according to the instructions on the package. Let the cookies cool.

5. Put ¼ cup frosting in a plastic bag. Seal the bag. Cut one corner of the bag to make a small hole.

6. Gently **squeeze** the bag until frosting comes out of the hole. Use it to draw lines of frosting along the lines made in the cookies.

TASTY ANGLES 🔥

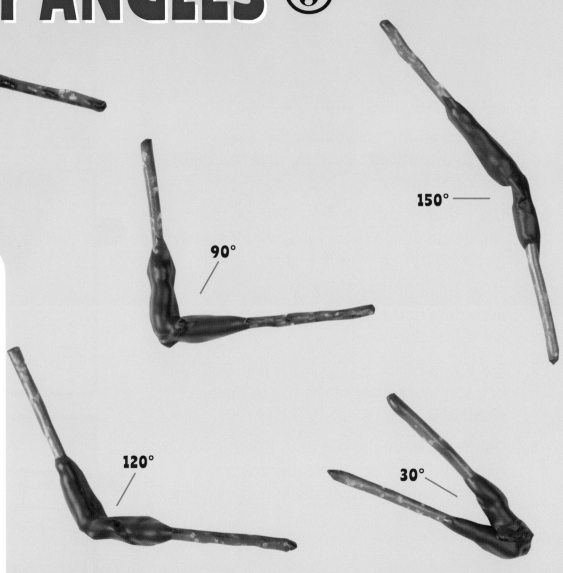

60°

150°

90°

120°

30°

INGREDIENTS

- ½ cup chocolate chips
- pretzel sticks

TOOLS

- marker
- paper
- protractor
- wax paper
- tape
- measuring cups
- microwave-safe bowl
- oven mitts
- spoon

When two lines meet, they form an angle. Angles are measured in **degrees**. Look for examples of angles around your school and home. Then make your own angles to eat!

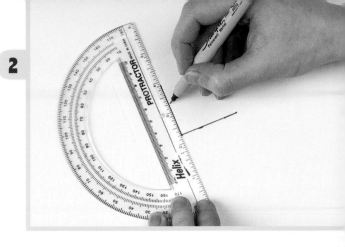

1. Draw a straight line on a sheet of paper. Set the protractor along the line. Make a mark above the protractor at the 90-degree point.

2. Draw a straight line between the mark and the end of the line. This creates a 90-degree angle. This is called a right angle.

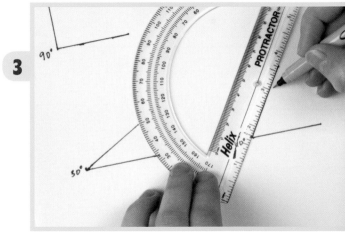

3. Repeat steps 1 and 2 to draw 30-degree and 60-degree angles on the paper. These are acute angles.

4. Repeat steps 1 and 2 to draw 120-degree and 150-degree angles. These are obtuse angles.

5. Place a sheet of wax paper on top of the paper with angles drawn on it. Tape the wax paper to the table to hold it in place.

Continued on the next page.

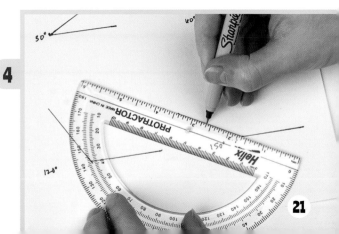

7

9

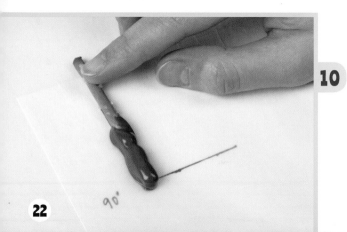

10

6. Put the chocolate chips in a microwave-safe bowl.

7. Microwave the chocolate chips for 30 seconds. Stir.

8. Repeat step 7 until the chocolate is fully melted.

9. Dip the end of a pretzel stick into the melted chocolate.

10. Place the pretzel on the wax paper over one line of an angle. The chocolate-coated end should be at the point where the two lines meet.

11. Repeat steps 9 and 10 for the other line of the angle.

12. Spoon a little extra melted chocolate onto the point where the pretzel sticks meet.

13. Repeat steps 9 through 12 for the rest of the angles. Let the chocolate harden before eating the angles!

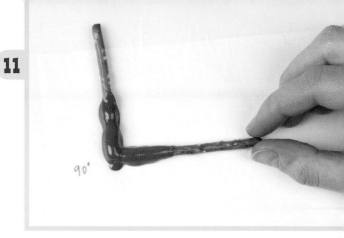

LOOK FOR ANGLES IN THESE AND OTHER COMMON OBJECTS!

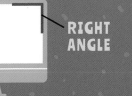

RIGHT ANGLE

OBTUSE ANGLE

ACUTE ANGLE

TANGRAM SANDWICH

INGREDIENTS
- bread
- sandwich fillings (peanut butter, jelly, Nutella, marshmallow fluff)

TOOLS
- dinner knife
- ruler

A tangram is a Chinese puzzle made of seven **geometric** shapes. The challenge is to arrange the shapes to form a figure or object. What can you create with your tangram sandwich?

1. | Spread your chosen fillings on two **slices** of bread.

2. Press the slices of bread together to make a sandwich. Cut the crusts off the sandwich.

3. | Cut the sandwich into a perfect square. Make the square as large as the bread size will allow. Measure the sides to make sure they are the same length.

4. | Cut the sandwich according to the illustration on the next page.

5. Use the tangram pieces to form the figures and objects. See some examples of tangram patterns on page 27 for inspiration!

Continued on the next page.

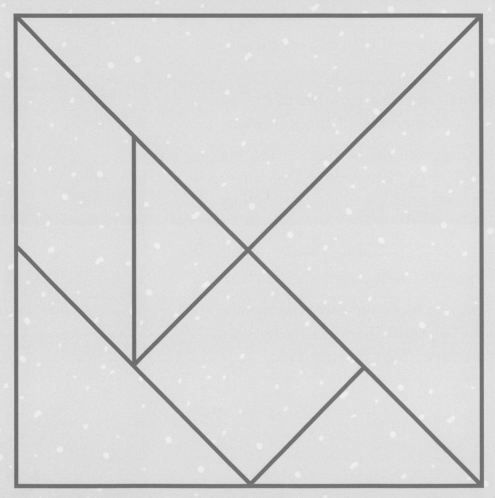

HOW TO CUT A SQUARE INTO TANGRAM PIECES

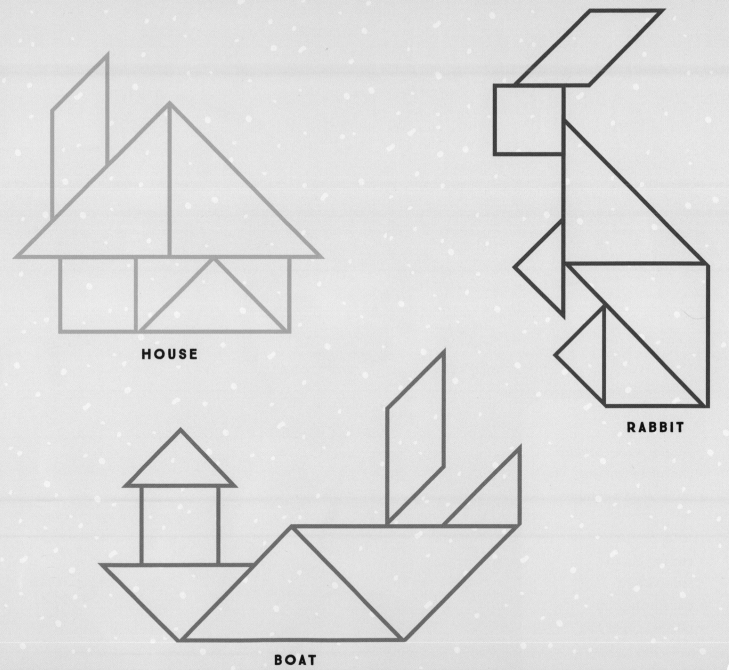

HOUSE

RABBIT

BOAT

27

DELICIOUS DOMINOES

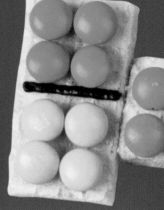
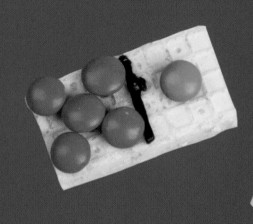

INGREDIENTS

- vanilla wafer cookies
- chocolate frosting
- mini M&M's candies

TOOLS

- cutting board
- sharp knife
- measuring cup
- plastic zipper bag
- scissors

Dominoes are game pieces that originated in China hundreds of years ago. There are many different games you can play with dominoes. Enjoy a game and a snack with your own set of domino cookies!

1. Cut a wafer cookie in half crosswise to make two domino tiles. Cut more cookies in half until you have as many tiles as you'd like.

2. Put ¼ cup chocolate frosting in a plastic bag. Seal the bag. Cut one corner of the bag to make a small hole.

3. Gently **squeeze** the bag until frosting comes out of the hole. Use it to draw a line across each tile. This divides each tile into two sections.

4. Draw a pattern of zero to five dots in each tile section.

5. Place a mini M&M on each dot of frosting.

6. Have an adult help you find the rules for dominoes games online. Play a game with your friends. Then eat the dominoes!

29

CONCLUSION

Math is the science of numbers. Mathematicians study numbers in quantities, shapes, measurements, and more. Today, math is used for **complicated** operations, such as space travel and GPS **navigation**.

MAKING SNACKS IS JUST ONE WAY TO LEARN ABOUT MATH. HOW WILL YOU CONTINUE YOUR MATH ADVENTURE?

QUIZ

1. WHO IS KNOWN FOR CREATING THE FIRST DIGITAL CALCULATOR?

2. MATH IS USED TO FORECAST THE WEATHER. TRUE OR FALSE?

3. WHAT IS AN ANGLE THAT IS LESS THAN 90 DEGREES CALLED?

LEARN MORE ABOUT IT!

YOU CAN FIND OUT MORE ABOUT MATH AT THE LIBRARY. OR YOU CAN ASK AN ADULT TO HELP YOU FIND INFORMATION ABOUT MATH ON THE INTERNET!

ANSWERS: 1. BLAISE PASCAL 2. TRUE 3. ACUTE

GLOSSARY

algorithm – a set of steps for solving a mathematical problem or completing a computer process.

calculate – to find an answer using a mathematical process. The process is called a calculation. A device that performs calculations is a calculator.

complicated – having many parts, details, ideas, or functions.

degree – a unit used to measure the size of an angle.

geometry – a branch of mathematics that deals with lines, angles, surfaces, and solids. Something related to geometry is geometric.

munch – to chew or eat.

navigation – the process of planning how to get somewhere.

permission – when a person in charge says it's okay to do something.

scholar – a person who studies one or more subjects for a long time.

slice – a thin piece cut from something.

squeeze – to press the sides of something together.

symbol – a character or picture used instead of a word.